THE ULTIMATE DREAMWORKS COOKBOOK

EDDA USA

THE ULTIMATE DREAMWORKS COOKBOOK

Authors: Edda USA Editorital Team, Cynthia Littlefield
and Judy Katschke
Photographer: Gassi.is
Layout and design: Olafur Gudlaugsson
Cover design: Olafur Gudlaugsson
Printed in Slovenia

Distributed by Macmillan

ISBN: 978-1-94078-726-8

www.eddausa.com

WELCOME

What do Shrek, Po, Hiccup, Alex, and all of your favorite DreamWorks Animation pals have in common? They love adventure, loads of laughs and awesome stuff to eat. The Ultimate DreamWorks Cookbook is filled with delicious character-inspired recipes to satisfy the most adventurous appetites, and are as fun to make as they are to eat! You'll find everything from fresh fruits with a "Wild" Madagascar twist and a Croodaceous quiche, to heaping helpings of pancakes fit for a Dragon Warrior and hearty sandwiches for ogre-sized cravings. Don't worry if you're new to cooking. Remember, the Croods were new to fire once but now they can't live without it! With easy-to-follow, step-by-step instructions and color photos of each recipe, cooking has never been so fun. And in the worlds of your DreamWorks friends, fun always rules.

GETTING STARTED

Before the mixes can be mixed and the dishes can be dished, here are some important tips to remember:

Always ask a parent for permission to start a cooking adventure. Better still, ask a parent to join you in the kitchen!

Always wash your hands.

Wear appropriate clothing. An apron around your waist and sleeves pushed up to your elbows helps to keep your clothes from collecting spills. If you have long hair, tie it back or use a cap. Even Shrek doesn't like hair in his food.

Be organized. Make sure to read the whole recipe before beginning and have all the needed equipment gathered, such as measuring spoon, bowls etc.

Have all the ingredients ready.

Make sure to have an adult help you with all electrical equipment, such as stoves, ovens, blenders or mixers.

Never use knives and scissors without an adult present.

Have fun!

BREAKFAST

Breakfast is the most important meal of the day even in the swamp. But to Shrek it's also the messiest, especially when Donkey takes over the kitchen. Lucky for Shrek, Donkey's stack of delicious waffles topped with syrup and berries are worth the wait...and the mess.

PO'S AWESOME PANCAKES

As much as Po loves kung fu, he might just love food a little bit more. As Dragon Warrior he needs a lot of energy to tackle the difficult exercises that Master Shifu schedules every day for him and the Furious Five! He must start the day with a meal that is both nutritious and energizing in order to keep his kung fu skills honed. A hearty, homemade plate of pancakes is just what Po needs.

INGREDIENTS

Makes 12 pancakes

2 large eggs, beaten
1¼ cups milk
1 teaspoon vanilla extract
1½ cups all-purpose flour
1 tablespoon baking powder
1 teaspoon granulated sugar
½ teaspoons salt
2 tablespoons butter, softened,
for the batter
1 tablespoon butter
for frying

**Serves 4
Prep time
15 min.
Cooking time
45 min.**

INSTRUCTIONS

1. Whisk together the eggs, milk, and vanilla extract in a large mixing bowl.

2. In a separate smaller bowl, whisk together the flour, baking powder, sugar, and salt.

3. Add the 2 tablespoons of cooled melted butter and the flour mixture to the egg mixture. Stir just until the ingredients are combined and the batter is still a little lumpy.

4. Heat a griddle over medium-high heat and melt the last tablespoon of butter on it.

5. Use a measuring cup to pour ¼ cup of batter per pancake onto the griddle.

6. Cook the pancakes until little bubbles rise in the batter before flipping them with a spatula. Let the pancakes cook for another minute or so, removing them from the griddle when the bottoms are the same golden brown as the tops.

7. Serve the pancakes warm with extra butter and maple syrup.

Skadoosh! You've just been served...breakfast.

SHiFU'S SECRET SUN TOAST

If you think that Master Shifu has his hands full when training Po and the Furious Five, you're right. That's why he keeps a strict regimen of training, discipline and diet. He must also prepare his kung fu warriors for any situation, and help keep them healthy and strong. One of his secrets is Sun Toast!

INGREDIENTS

Makes 4 slices

4 slices bread
4 teaspoons butter
4 medium or large eggs
½ cup grated cheddar cheese
Salt and ground black pepper to taste

**Serves 4
Prep time
5 min.
Cooking time
5 min.**

INSTRUCTIONS

1. Use a round cookie cutter or the rim of a small drinking glass to cut a hole about 3 inches wide in the middle of each bread slice. (Save the cutouts to make fresh breadcrumbs, if you like.)

2. Melt 1 teaspoon of the butter in a frying pan over medium heat and then place a slice of bread on top of it.

3. Crack one egg into the hole in the bread. Cook the sun toast until the bread is lightly browned and the egg is cooked on one side.

4. Use a spatula to flip the bread-and-egg over. Now sprinkle on Shifu's secret ingredient: 2 tablespoons of the grated cheese.

5. Continue to cook the sun toast until the egg yolk is almost set. Then season it with salt and pepper.

6. Make three more sun toasts with the remaining bread slices, eggs, and cheese.

Now you're ready to enjoy a breakfast any one of the Furious Five would "flip" over.

FIONA'S FEISTY OMELET

Princess Fiona has a lot to do. Not only does she have to help Shrek maintain the swamp but she also has the triplets to think about. Those little bundles of joy need constant nurturing and their appetite is voracious! Fiona's Feisty Omelet is a nutritious and stomach-filling omelet that will help any sweet darlings grow into strong ogres!

INGREDIENTS

1 tablespoon butter

½ cup sliced white mushrooms

1 tablespoon sliced scallions

3 large eggs

¼–½ cup grated mozzarella cheese

Salt and ground black pepper to taste

Serves 2
Prep time 10 min.
Cooking time 5-10 min.

INSTRUCTIONS

1. Melt the butter in a frying pan over medium heat. Gently stir the mushrooms into the melted butter.

2. When the mushrooms turn golden on the edges, stir in the scallions.

3. Beat together the eggs and salt and pepper in a small mixing bowl. Pour the eggs over the mushroom mixture, spreading them evenly in the pan.

4. When the egg is almost cooked through, sprinkle the cheese on top.

5. Fold the omelet in half, slide it onto a plate, and serve.

Growing ogres everywhere agree that this tasty omelet is all it's cracked up to be!

DONKEY'S WAFFLES

There's no stopping Donkey when he starts talking. But once upon a time Shrek had an idea: if he couldn't close Donkey's mouth he would fill it with his favorite treat—waffles. Before long Shrek's best friend was sinking his sweet tooth into a tasty, towering stack. Donkey never dreamed Shrek could make waffles. Now he's a believer!

INGREDIENTS

Makes four 6-inch-round waffles

2 cups all-purpose flour

2 tablespoons granulated sugar

4 teaspoons baking powder

½ teaspoon salt

2 medium eggs

1¾ cups milk

½ cup butter, melted

1 teaspoon vanilla extract

Cooking spray

Serves 4
Prep time
20 min.
Cooking time
15-20 min.

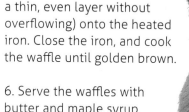

INSTRUCTIONS

1. Preheat a waffle iron. If you do not own a waffle iron you can use a grill pan with great results!

2. Whisk together the flour, sugar, baking powder, and salt in a small mixing bowl.

3. In a large mixing bowl, hand-beat or whisk the eggs until fluffy.

4. Add the milk, melted butter, vanilla extract, and flour mixture to the eggs, and mix the batter just until smooth.

5. Spray the heated waffle iron with cooking spray. For each waffle, pour ¼ cup of batter (or enough to create a thin, even layer without overflowing) onto the heated iron. Close the iron, and cook the waffle until golden brown.

6. Serve the waffles with butter and maple syrup, fruit, or another one of your favorite toppings.

Shrek's plan worked. Well, sort of. If only Donkey would learn not to talk with his mouth full.

15

GLORIA'S GLORIOUS FRUIT SALAD

Gloria was just as accustomed to the relaxed routine of the zoo as her friends were when they were accidentally shipped off to Madagascar. Before that she never had to prepare her own food and she missed her daily breakfast of delicious fruit! But what do you know? When you're stranded on an exotic island full of fresh fruit, you learn that making your own glorious fruit salad isn't so hard!

INGREDIENTS

1 ripe mango, peeled, pitted, and cubed
6 cups seedless watermelon cubes
3 cups fresh pineapple cubes
1 banana, peeled and sliced
1 cup whipping cream
1 teaspoon vanilla extract
Fresh mint for garnish

Serves 2
Prep time 20 min.

INSTRUCTIONS

1. Combine all of the fruit cubes and slices in a large bowl, and stir gently to mix the salad.

2. Pour the whipping cream into a chilled mixing bowl. Add the vanilla extract. Whisk the cream until soft peaks form.

3. Spoon the fruit salad into serving dishes, top with the vanilla whipped cream and small sprigs of mint, and serve.

4. For lighter option you can skip the cream.

Of course, you can follow Gloria's lead and make this salad with just about any fruits you happen to find in season. Fresh berries are especially delicious tossed into the mix.

STOICK'S PERFECT PORRIDGE

Vikings are generally big and strong and Stoick is no exception! When he was a young lad his mother served him a bowl of steaming porridge every morning. Stoick gobbled down the bowl in a heartbeat and often helped himself to more until he finished the whole pot! It was this recipe that helped make Stoick into the strong and hardy leader of the Vikings.

INGREDIENTS

1 cup rolled oats

1 cup milk

1 cup water

¼ cup raisins

1 tablespoon honey

Optional add-in items can be other dried fruit, like cranberries and pumpkin.

Serves 1
Prep time
3 min.
Cooking time
5-8 min.

INSTRUCTIONS

1. Combine the oats, milk, and water in a small saucepan.

2. Bring the mixture to a boil over medium heat.

3. Reduce the heat and cook the porridge at a simmer for 4–5 minutes, stirring constantly to keep it from sticking to the bottom of the pan.

4. When the oatmeal is the desired consistency, mix in the raisins.

5. Spoon the porridge into a bowl, and drizzle the honey on top.

Finish the whole bowl to be strong like Stoick!

GRAN'S GRAND REFRESHER

"Still alive!" is Gran's usual saying. She is ancient beyond measure (some say she is 45!) and stubborn beyond belief. This crotchety old gal is as feisty as she is wrinkled. It may seem odd that her favorite drink in the morning is a refreshing tropical smoothie. But it's hard to chew with just one tooth!

INGREDIENTS

Serves 4
Prep time 15 min.

1 cup skimmed milk
½ cup water
⅔ cup plain yogurt
1½ cups diced pineapple
1 cup diced mango
1 ripe banana, sliced
½ ripe diced pear
1½ teaspoons honey
2–3 cups crushed ice

INSTRUCTIONS

1. Immerse 2 large glasses in cold water. Chill the wet glasses in the freezer to frost them while you prepare the refresher.

2. Pour the milk and water into the pitcher of a blender. Add the yogurt, pineapple, mango, banana, pear, and honey. Pulse the mixture a few times to blend the ingredients.

3. Add the ice to the mixture and blend until smooth.

4. Remove the glasses from the freezer, fill them, and serve.

Besides being naturally sweet and creamy, this delicious refresher is chock-full of nutrients to help keep you as energetic as Gran.

TIP'S START-THE-DAY PARFAIT

With the Gorg gone, Oh could finally do what he dreamed of doing since landing on Planet Earth—throw a fun-filled housewarming brunch. Wanting to make Oh feel at home, Tip brought a gift of her favorite morning meal: yogurt, fruit and granola layered in a colorful parfait. When the Boov tasted Tip's Start-the-Day Parfait they were tickled pink. How could anything on Earth taste better than a delicious football?

INGREDIENTS

1¼ cups plain yogurt
1½ teaspoons honey
3 tablespoons granola
Handful of raspberries
Handful of blueberries

**Serves 1
Prep time
5 min.**

INSTRUCTIONS

1. Stir together the yogurt and maple syrup in a small bowl.

2. Spoon a third of the sweetened yogurt into the bottom of a tall glass.

3. Add 1 tablespoon of the granola and all but a few of the raspberries to the glass.

4. Add another layer of the yogurt followed by another tablespoon of granola. Now, add all but a few of the blueberries.

5. Spoon in the rest of the yogurt, and top it with the remaining granola, raspberries, and blueberries.

The Boov were proven wrong, this truly tasted better than football.

24

LUNCH

When Po and the Furious Five engage in kung fu training they work up a serious sweat and a fierce appetite. So when it's time for these masters to refuel and skadoosh their hunger, they stop using their fists and feet and use their noodles to whip up wholesome lunches of awesomeness.

THE FURIOUS FIVE'S POWER PUNCH PANCAKES

The Furious Five are the most renowned kung fu warriors in all of China. They train daily in the martial arts, constantly striving for perfection. When they rest during lunch they must be conscious of getting the right nourishment for the rest of the day's exercises. With a delicious blend of eggs, vegetables and spices, Power Punch Pancakes are just what they need to keep kicking, punching, leaping and jumping!

INGREDIENTS

1 cup all-purpose flour
1 teaspoon baking powder
1 teaspoon onion powder
1 teaspoon garlic powder
2 eggs, lightly beaten
½ cup milk
2 cups grated carrot
1½ cups grated zucchini
1 cup spinach, thinly sliced
2 scallions, thinly sliced
1 tablespoon cooking oil
Salt and ground black pepper
to taste

**Serves 4
Prep time
20 min.
Cooking time
10 min.**

INSTRUCTIONS

1. Whisk together the flour, baking powder, onion powder, and garlic powder in a large mixing bowl.

2. Fold the eggs, milk, carrot, zucchini, spinach, and scallions into the flour mix until the batter is well blended.

3. Heat the oil in a large frying pan over medium heat.

4. Use a ¼-cup measuring cup to drop batter for each pancake onto the griddle, spacing them slightly apart. Use the back of a spoon to gently press the batter into pancake shapes.

5. Fry the pancakes until the bottoms are golden brown (about 3 minutes), then use a spatula to flip them. Continue cooking the pancakes until the flip sides are golden, about 3 more minutes or so.

6. Transfer the pancakes to a serving platter, and allow them to cool for a minute. Then season them with salt and pepper, and serve.

These lunchtime pancakes are packed with plenty of nutrients to keep even kung fu warriors-in-training on the go.

MASTER TIGRESS' TOFU TOSS

Master Tigress is the ultimate warrior. Few are more dedicated in their pursuit of excellence in the art of kung fu, and none fiercer in battle or more courageous. Tigress constantly needs to replenish her energy and yet stay light and strong. A tasty blend of herbs and tofu, stir-fried in soy sauce and Asian spices can help seasoned masters as well as young warriors new to the kung fu scene become strong.

INGREDIENTS

Teriyaki Sauce
1 cup rice vinegar
1 cup white grape juice
½ cup sugar
1 cup soy sauce
2 teaspoons ground ginger
1 teaspoon garlic powder
3 tablespoons water
3 tablespoons cornstarch

Tofu Toss
14–ounce (1pkg) extra-firm tofu
Sesame oil for frying
⅓ cup sliced carrot
⅓ cup sliced red bell pepper
1 head bok choy cut into 8 pieces
½ cup bean sprouts
Salt and pepper to taste
Lemon juice to taste

**Serves 4
Prep time
20-30 min.
Cooking time
10 min.**

INSTRUCTIONS

Teriyaki Sauce

1. Combine the rice vinegar and grape juice in a large pot, and boil the mixture for 2–3 minutes.

2. Stir in the sugar, soy sauce, ginger, and garlic powder. Bring the mixture back to a boil then lower the heat and cook the sauce at a simmer.

3. In a small bowl or cup, stir together the water and cornstarch and then stir the mixture into the sauce.

4. Continue simmering the teriyaki sauce until it thickens. Remove the pan from the heat.

Tofu Toss

1. Set the tofu on a piece of paper towel to dry. Then cut it into small bite-size cubes.

2. Heat a little bit of sesame oil in a large frying pan or a wok over medium heat. Fry the tofu on all sides until golden. Transfer the tofu to a plate, and set it aside for now.

3. In the same pan or wok, fry the carrot, bell pepper, and bok choy until soft, stirring the whole time.

4. Add the teriyaki sauce to the pan, and continue to cook the vegetables for 2–3 minutes.

5. Now add the tofu cubes to the pan, stir to coat everything with the teriyaki sauce, and cook the mixture for another 2 minutes.

6. Season the mixture with salt, ground black pepper, and lemon juice.

Packed with a flavorful kick, Master Tigress' Tofu Toss is one of the most popular dishes on the Jade Palace menu.

29

MR. PING'S SECRET NOODLE SOUP

In the Valley of Peace, what's a bigger secret than performing the Wuxi Finger Hold? Mr. Ping's secret noodle soup! One day, curious Po set out to discover his dad's top-secret ingredient. First the Dragon Warrior hid behind a panda-sized bag of flour. Next he peeked out to watch his dad cook. Were noodles the secret ingredient? Nah...nothing secret about noodles. Was it celery? Nope. Celery didn't cut it. Onions? For crying out loud—that couldn't be it. Po was about to give up when Mr. Ping began to sing. And shake his feathery tail. And smile as he stirred the pot. Po smiled and it finally clicked. The secret ingredient wasn't noodles, or celery, or onions. It was that Mr. Ping believed it was special. (Well, that, and the fun Mr. Ping was having while cooking the soup!)

INGREDIENTS

1 tablespoon olive oil
1 cup sliced celery
1 cup peeled sliced carrots
½ cup diced yellow onion
2 garlic cloves, minced
1 dried shiitake mushroom, crushed
4 cups chicken broth
8 ounces egg noodles
Salt, ground black pepper and lemon juice to taste

**Serves 4
Prep time
15 min.
Cooking time
20-30 min.**

INSTRUCTIONS

1. Heat the oil in a soup pot over medium heat, and sauté the celery, carrots, onion, garlic, and mushroom in it until soft.

2. Pour in the chicken broth and bring it to boil.

3. Add the noodles to the pot and simmer them until cooked.

4. Season the soup with salt, pepper and lemon juice.

Just like Po has mastered kung fu, he's also mastered slurping! The Furious Five can hear him all the way up in the Jade Palace.

SHREK'S OOEY-GOOEY OGRE-THE-TOP SANDWICH

Shrek seems to be constantly interrupted and forced to leave his swamp to save the kingdom, rescue the princess, or help out Donkey! There never seems to be a quiet moment to enjoy the muddy pit he calls home. Shrek needs to keep up his energy before heading out to save the day. Here's a classic sandwich recipe to help a hungry hero tackle every adventure.

INGREDIENTS

2 slices of bread

2–3 slices of cheese (American, cheddar, mozzarella or provolone)

2 slices of ham

1 pineapple ring, grilled (tomatoes can be used instead)

1½ teaspoons butter, softened

Serves 1
Prep time 5 min.
Cooking time 10 min.

INSTRUCTIONS

1. Place one of the bread slices on a flat surface, and top it with 1–1½ slices of cheese.

2. Next, layer on the 2 ham slices, the grilled pineapple ring, and the remaining cheese.

3. Spread half of the butter on one side of the second bread slice. Then set the slice atop the sandwich fillings, buttered side up.

4. Melt the remaining butter in a small frying pan over medium heat. Lower the heat, and carefully set the sandwich in the pan. Cover the pan, and grill the sandwich for 2½–3 minutes.

5. Use a spatula to flip the sandwich. Gently press down on the top to stick the filling together. Re-cover the pan, and grill the sandwich until the cheese is melted, about 2–3 more minutes.

6. Transfer the grilled sandwich to a plate, slice it in half, and it's ready to eat.

When Shrek is feeling extra adventurous he likes to add different ingredients to the sandwich, such as bugs, slugs and weedrat. But you might prefer items like bacon, tomatoes or avocado.

PUSS IN BOOTS' PURR-FECT TUNA PASTA

The famous romantic adventurer, Puss In Boots, is a gourmet cat of the classical kind. After a morning of some adventuring and swordplay he loves to sit down and nibble on a great meal, preferably something with fish in it! Being suave and sophisticated, Puss In Boots adores Italian cuisine. This Tuna Pasta is something any cool cat will cherish.

INGREDIENTS

2 cups uncooked macaroni

1 tablespoon cooking oil

2 garlic cloves, finely chopped

2 shallots, finely chopped

1 (5-ounce) can of tuna, drained and flaked

3 cups milk

1 cup cream cheese

½ cup cooked sweet corn

1 teaspoon red pepper flakes

Salt and ground black pepper to taste

½–¾ cup grated mozzarella cheese

**Serves 4
Prep time
20 min.
Cooking time
45-55 min.**

INSTRUCTIONS

1. Cook the macaroni according to the package directions. Then drain it and set it aside to cool.

2. Preheat the oven to 350° F.

3. Meanwhile, heat the cooking oil in a large saucepan over medium heat. Cook the garlic and shallots in it, gently stirring, until soft.

4. Add the tuna, milk, and cream cheese. Continue cooking and stirring until the cream cheese is melted.

5. Stir in the sweet corn and red pepper flakes.

Season the mixture with salt and pepper.

6. Combine the macaroni and sauce in a 2½ or 3-quart casserole dish.

7. Top the macaroni with the grated mozzarella, and bake the casserole in the oven until the top turns golden brown and the sauce is bubbling (about 35–45 minutes).

By savoring this dish, you might inherit some of Puss' charm and elegance.

HICCUP'S HEROIC BLT

Vikings don't live on fish and bread alone. So one day Hiccup came up with a recipe and a plan. He and his fellow Dragon Riders set off with their dragons on a quest for inventive new dishes. Toothless helped to bring home the bacon. Astrid and Stormfly swooped down to scoop up juicy tomatoes. With Snotlout on his back, Hookfang got his hooks in some lettuce. Even Fishlegs and Meatlug got into the groove hauling back crunchy rocks. The results: bacon, lettuce and tomato sandwiches cooked on a hot-rock grill. Hiccup knew his BLTs would be a hit. He also knew the most important ingredient of all: teamwork!

INGREDIENTS

8 strips bacon
Mayonnaise to taste
3 slices toasted bread
4 large iceberg lettuce leaves
Medium heirloom tomato, sliced
Ground black pepper to taste

Serves 1
Prep time
8 min.
Cooking time
15 min.

INSTRUCTIONS

1. Fry the bacon in a pan over medium-high heat, turning the strips over to crisp them on both sides. Drain the bacon on a paper towel-lined plate.

2. Spread mayonnaise on one side of a single slice of the toasted bread.

3. Top the toast slice with 2 of the lettuce leaves, half the tomato slices, 4 strips of bacon, and a second slice of toast. Spread more mayonnaise on the top of the second toast slice.

4. Add the remaining lettuce and tomato, and season the tomato slices with ground black pepper.

5. Add the remaining 4 strips of bacon, and top the sandwich with the third slice of toast.

Leave it to Hiccup to have a hunch that changes the way Vikings view lunch!

TOOTHLESS' FAVORITE FISH BITES

There was a time when Hiccup and the other Vikings of Berk had absolutely no idea about the dragons' taste for all things fishy. Little did they know that the dragons were stealing the sheep to keep themselves safe, not to eat for lunch. All the Vikings had to do to keep the dragons happy was to prepare a fresh catch from the ocean. This recipe is a favorite of Toothless, who can gobble down those fish bites by the dozen. An excellent meal for any dragon—and Dragon Rider!

INGREDIENTS

Fish Bites
1 pound white fish (cod, haddock, tilapia, or another favorite variety)
½ medium yellow onion, minced
1 medium or large egg, lightly beaten
1 cup milk
2 tablespoons all-purpose flour
1½ tablespoons cornstarch
1 teaspoon salt
1 teaspoon ground black pepper
1 tablespoon butter

Tartar Sauce
½ cup mayonnaise
1 teaspoon sweet relish
1 teaspoon minced onion
1½ teaspoons fresh lemon juice

Serves 4
Prep time
45 min.
Cooking time
25 min.

INSTRUCTIONS

1. Use a grinder or a food processor to mince the fish. Or, if you prefer, simply use a kitchen knife to finely chop the fish.

2. Combine the fish, onion, egg, and milk in a mixing bowl.

3. Sprinkle the flour, cornstarch, salt, and pepper into the bowl. Stir until all the ingredients are evenly mixed.

4. Shape tablespoons of the mixture into small round balls. You should have 12–15 fish bites when you're done.

5. Melt the butter in a frying pan over medium-high heat. Arrange the fish bites in the pan, and cook them until the bottoms turn golden brown. Flip the bites over, and continue frying them until cooked through and golden brown all over.

6. Mix together all of the tartar sauce ingredients in a small serving bowl. Serve the sauce with the cooked fish bites.

Eat up! You don't need to be a dragon to enjoy this scrumptious fish dish.

SANDY'S CRAZY QUICHE

One day the Croods spent hours chasing after a giant egg. But just as Eep was about to make the winning catch, a Macawnivore swooped in and grabbed the egg between its tusks. The prehistoric pest buzzed off until—crack! The shell split spilling gooey yoke inside a deep mammoth footprint below. Sandy, the baby Crood, had a wild time tossing every yummy thing she could find into the mix. With a little help from the sun, the egg and fillings were baked to perfection. And the Croods enjoyed their first crazy quiche.

INGREDIENTS

Pre-made pastry dough
(enough for a single 12-inch pie crust)

2 cups grated Gruyère cheese

1 teaspoon all-purpose flour

4 large eggs, beaten

1 cup heavy cream

1 cup cooked asparagus, cut into
1-inch pieces

1½ teaspoons salt

1 teaspoon ground black pepper

Serves 4
Prep time
20 min.
Cooking time
45-60 min.

INSTRUCTIONS

1. Preheat the oven to 350° F.

2. Working on a flour-dusted surface with a flour-dusted rolling pin, roll out the pie pastry into a circle approximately ⅛ inch thick and large enough to drape over a 12-inch quiche pan or pie plate.

3. Gently press the rolled pastry down into the quiche pan, making sure the edges cover the rim. Pinch the dough around the rim to create a crimped border. This will help keep the filling from overflowing.

4. Toss together the cheese and the flour in a small bowl.

5. In a separate bowl, combine the eggs, cream, asparagus, salt, and pepper. Stir in the cheese mixture.

6. Pour the filling into the pastry-lined pan.

7. Bake the quiche until the filling is golden and firm to the touch, about 45–60 minutes.

Quiche may sound super fancy but to Sandy it's as easy as pie.

41

TIP'S HOME-Y HOTDOGS

When Oh made his ingenious adjustments to Tip's car he added a few nifty parts. One of those great tricks resulted in mouth-watering hot dogs to go along with those sweet Slushies. Here are three classic ways to make those interstellar hot dogs yourself!

THE CHILI DOG

INGREDIENTS

1 tablespoon cooking oil
8 ounces ground beef
½ cup sliced red onion, plus extra
to use as a topping
1 (28-ounce) can crushed tomatoes
1 tablespoon chili powder
½ teaspoon ground black pepper
4 hot dogs
½ cup water
4 hot dog buns
2 ounces sharp cheddar cheese
2 pickles, sliced

Serves 4
Prep time
15 min.
Cooking time
10-90 min.

INSTRUCTIONS

1. Heat the oil in a frying pan over medium heat. Add the beef and break it up with a wooden spoon or spatula.

2. Add the onion to the pan, and stir it and the beef until the meat browns. Remove the pan from the heat

3. Combine the tomatoes, chili powder, and pepper in a pot over medium heat, stirring to mix.

4. Add the cooked beef and onion to the tomatoes, and simmer the sauce, stirring occasionally, until it is very thick, about 1½ hours.

5. Shortly before serving, boil the hot dogs in the ½ cup of water until heated through.

6. While the hot dogs cook, warm the hot dog buns in the oven for 4 minutes or so.

7. Place the hot dogs in the warm buns, and spoon the chili sauce on top of them. Sprinkle on the cheddar cheese, remaining chopped red onion, and sliced pickles.

THE BLT DOG

INGREDIENTS

1 cup mayonnaise
1 tablespoon pickle relish
1½ teaspoons dry parsley
1½ teaspoons dry chives
1½ teaspoons dry tarragon
4 hot dogs
½ cup water
4 hot dog buns
4 strips cooked bacon
1 large tomato, sliced
4 cups shredded iceberg lettuce
⅓ cup shredded fresh basil leaves

Serves 4
Prep time 15 min.
Cooking time 10-90 min.

INSTRUCTIONS

1. In a small bowl, whisk together the mayonnaise, relish, parsley, chives, chervil, and tarragon until you have a smooth remoulade sauce.

2. Boil the hot dogs in the ½ cup of water until heated through.

3. While the hot dogs cook, warm the hot dog buns in the oven for 4 minutes or so.

4. Place the hot dogs in the warm buns. Neatly arrange the bacon and tomato slices on top.

5. In a clean bowl, toss together the lettuce, basil, and some of the remoulade.

6. Top the dogs with the lettuce slaw, and serve them with the remaining remoulade on the side.

THE NYC HOTDOG

INGREDIENTS

1 cup chopped yellow onion
¼ cup fresh lemon juice
1 tablespoon brown sugar
³/₄ teaspoon cumin
½ teaspoon spicy mustard, plus more for topping the cooked hot dogs
1 teaspoon ketchup
Salt to taste
4 hot dogs
½ cup water
4 hot dog buns

**Serves 4
Prep time
15 min.
Cooking time
10-90 min.**

INSTRUCTIONS

1. Prepare an onion relish by combing the yellow onion, lemon juice, brown sugar, cumin, mustard, ketchup and salt in a small pot over medium heat.

2. Bring the mixture to a boil, stirring frequently. Immediately remove the pot from the heat and set the relish aside.

3. Boil the hot dogs in the ½ cup of water until heated through.

4. While the hot dogs cook, warm the hot dog buns in the oven for 4 minutes or so.

5. Place the hot dogs in the warm buns. Top them with onion relish, spicy mustard, and sauerkraut. Serve at once.

Tip and Oh don't agree on much, but they do agree on this: these dressed-up dogs are out of this world!

SNACKS 'N' DRINKS

No matter how far they roam Alex, Marty, Melman and Gloria are Central Park Zoosters through and through. But these New Yorkers don't live on pizza, bagels and pretzels alone. Their travels bring them wild adventure and exotic recipes for snacks and drinks. They're not just delicious—they're freshilicious!

VIPER'S VEGGIE DIP

As one of the Furious Five, Viper is constantly training. So she seriously needs to have some healthy snacks between meals! She prefers something light and filled with protein for her muscles. The Veggie Dip with pita chips is the perfect snack to keep up the energy levels of this, as Po says, snickety snake!

INGREDIENTS

7 ounces plain hummus

6 ounces plain Greek yogurt

½ cup crumbled feta cheese

1 tablespoon lemon juice

½ teaspoon salt

½ teaspoon ground black pepper

1 large tomato, seeded and diced

2 tablespoons green olives, pitted and chopped

Bowl of pita chips

Large cucumber, sliced

Large red bell pepper, seeded and sliced

**Serves 4
Prep time
5 min.**

INSTRUCTIONS

1. Stir together the hummus, yogurt, feta cheese, and lemon juice in a medium-size serving bowl.

2. Sprinkle the salt and pepper onto the hummus. Then fold the tomato and green olives into the mixture until the vegetables and seasonings are evenly distributed.

3. Serve the hummus with the pita chips, cucumber, and red bell pepper.

One of Po's idols, Viper knows what it takes to be well-fueled for action!

KING JULIEN'S
FRUIT EXTRAVAGANZA

King Julien loves to move it, move it. So when his ringtail lemur started dragging on the Conga Line he knew he was losing juice. What's a pooped-out ruler to do? If you're King Julien, the answer is obvious. Throw another party! A Bring-Your-Own-Fruits party. At his command, King Julien was presented with pineapple, strawberries, grapes, coconuts—and because Madagascar grows a ton of cocoa—cocoa chips. In the shake of a feathery crown every last lemur began partying with rainbow-colored, chocolate-dipped fruit kabobs fit for a king.

INGREDIENTS

3 cups fresh pineapple cubes
20 strawberries
40 grapes
10 ounces dark chocolate or
2 cups semi sweet chocolate chips
4 ounces coconut flakes

**Serves 5
Prep time
15 min.
Cooking time
5 min.**

INSTRUCTIONS

1. Spread the coconut flakes on a flat dish.

2. Create fruit kabobs, by pushing individual pieces of fruit onto small wooden kitchen skewers, alternating the different types.

3. Set a heatproof bowl atop a pot of barely simmering water. Add the chocolate to the bowl, and stir regularly until it melts and blends into a smooth sauce. Be sure to use a dry spoon — even a little bit of water can stiffen the chocolate.

4. Cover your work surface with waxed paper. Working with one kabob at a time, drizzle some of the melted chocolate over the fruit. Roll the kabob in the coconut flakes while the chocolate is still warm, and set it on a waxed paper-lined tray.

5. When all the fruit spears are coated with chocolate
and coconut, chill them briefly before serving.

After munching on all that juicy fruit, King Julien is back to being the Monarch with the Most...the most energy, that is.

GUY'S PREHISTORIC "POPCORN"

When family night rolls around, Grug has a rule: all Croods gather to view the latest blockbuster cave painting while passing the crispy, fried scorpion legs. To elevate their viewing experience Guy stumbled across some unique combinations of ingredients and ultimately came upon a savory cave-watching snack made with cauliflower and Parmesan cheese.

INGREDIENTS

1 large head of cauliflower
4 tablespoons Parmesan cheese
2 tablespoons onion powder
2 teaspoons sea salt
1 teaspoon paprika
1 teaspoon ground black pepper
1 teaspoon granulated sugar
½ teaspoon garlic powder
3 tablespoons olive oil

Serves 2
Prep time
15 min.
Cooking time
15-20 min.

INSTRUCTIONS

1. Preheat the oven to 400° F.

2. Wash the cauliflower and cut it into small florets. Arrange the florets on a baking sheet lined with parchment paper.

3. Mix together the Parmesan cheese, onion powder, salt, paprika, pepper, sugar, and garlic powder in a small bowl.

4. Drizzle the olive oil onto the cauliflower. Then sprinkle on the cheese-and-spice mixture. Stir the florets until evenly coated.

5. Roast the cauliflower in the oven until golden brown, about 15–20 minutes.

One bite of this prehistoric "popcorn," and you're bound to agree—Guy has a real gift for getting others to see things in a brand new way.

OH'S SLUSHIOUS SMOOTHIE!

Who knew Slushies could be the perfect boost? Oh did, when he used one to power up Tip's mom's car. Thanks to a little Boov ingenuity Tip and her alien pal took to the sky on sweet Slushie fuel. Oh was happy to help and is sure to keep making this yummy-licious Slushious Smoothie in his new home on Earth.

INGREDIENTS

1 mango, peeled, seeded
and cut into chunks

1 banana, peeled and chopped

1 orange, peeled and chopped

1 cup nonfat plain yogurt

7 ice cubes

**Serves 2
Prep time
5 min.**

INSTRUCTIONS

1. Immerse two plastic cups in cold water.

2. Place the wet plastic cups in the freezer so they will turn frosty while you prepare the smoothie.

3. Combine the mango, banana, orange, yogurt, and ice cubes in the pitcher of a blender, and blend them until smooth.

4. Remove the glasses from the freezer and fill them with the smoothie mixture.

These Slushies are Oh-so-tasty and fun to drink.

DINNER

The Dragon Riders of Berk work hard at training dragons and discovering new worlds. They also work up huge appetites and huge appetites mean huge dinners. Lucky for Hiccup and his friends their helpful dragons are always there to help them fish and fire up the pits. Now that's a smokin' smorgasbord!

PO'S BODACIOUS DUMPLINGS

Master Shifu discovered Po's magnificent kung fu abilities when Po was after some dumplings. Just the sight of those delicious bites of heaven sent Po into a state of total awesomeness! No matter how Master Shifu tried to keep him at bay, Po always found new kung fu moves to get to those scrumptious little dumplings!

INGREDIENTS

Makes 50 dumplings

**Serves 4
Prep time
45 min.
Cooking time
5-8 min.**

Dumplings
½ pound ground beef
½ pound ground pork
1 medium egg, beaten
4 garlic cloves, minced
2 tablespoon minced fresh ginger
2 tablespoon sesame oil
2 tablespoon soy sauce
1 tablespoon finely chopped chives
1 teaspoon minced chili (optional)
50 dumpling or wonton wrappers
(sold in Asian specialty markets)
Olive oil for frying
1 cup water

Dipping Sauce
1 cup soy sauce
3 tablespoons rice vinegar
2 teaspoons toasted sesame seeds
1 teaspoon minced fresh ginger
1 teaspoon hot sauce

INSTRUCTIONS

1. To make the dumpling filling, mix together the ground beef, ground pork, egg, garlic, ginger, sesame oil, soy sauce, chives, and chili (if you're using it) in a large bowl until well combined.

2. Place a dumpling wrapper on a lightly floured surface. Spoon about 1 tablespoon of the filling onto the middle of the wrapper.

3. Wet the edge of the wrapper with a bit of water and then pinch the edges together, forming small pleats, to seal the dumpling.

4. Repeat steps 2 and 3 until all of the wrappers and filling are used.

5. Heat 1 tablespoon of olive oil in a frying pan over medium heat. Place 10–14 dumplings in the pan, making sure they do not touch each other. Cook the dumplings until golden, about 2 minutes per side.

6. Add ½ cup of water to the dumplings and simmer them, with the pan covered, until the filling is cooked through, about 6–8 minutes. Use a slotted spoon to transfer the dumplings to a covered serving dish to keep warm. Empty any remaining liquid from the pan.

7. Repeat steps 5 and 6 until all the dumplings are cooked.

8. To prepare the dipping sauce, simply stir together the soy sauce, vinegar, sesame seeds, ginger, and hot sauce in a small bowl.

It only takes a little taste to understand why the mere sight of these delectable dumplings sends Po into a food frenzy.

RISOTTO FIT FOR A FAIRY TALE

Fiona never missed her old life in Far, Far Away until she stumbled upon her old castle cookbook. There on the first page was the most regal recipe for Fiona's favorite dish: risotto. Would this savory rice dish be a five-burp meal for Shrek and the babies? Or would they ditch it for their usual raw onion and eyeball kabobs? There was only one way to find out. Princess Fiona would have to get cooking.

INGREDIENTS

1 tablespoon olive oil

½ pound fresh white mushrooms, sliced

4 skinless chicken breasts, cut into bite-size cubes

3 tablespoons butter

2 shallots, diced

2 garlic cloves, thinly sliced

1½ cups uncooked risotto rice

½ cup white grape juice

6 cups warm chicken stock

½ cup freshly grated Parmesan cheese

Salt and ground black pepper to taste

Serves 4
Prep time
25 min.
Cooking time
25 min.

INSTRUCTIONS

1. Heat the olive oil in a large frying pan over medium heat. Add the mushrooms and cook them until they turn golden. Add the cubed chicken and continue cooking, stirring occasionally, until the meat is fully cooked. Set the pan aside for now.

2. Melt the butter in a large heavy-bottomed pot over low heat. Add the shallots and garlic. Cook and stir them until soft, turning up the heat a bit if needed.

3. Add the rice to the pot, and cook it for 2 minutes, using a wooden spoon to stir the mixture with easy, even strokes to keep the grains from sticking to the pan.

4. Pour in the grape juice, continuing to stir, until the liquid is completely absorbed.

5. Stirring all the while, add ½ cup of the chicken stock and a sprinkling of the Parmesan. Repeat this step until the last of the stock is absorbed and all of the Parmesan is added. This should take about 15–20 minutes.

6. Remove the cooked rice from the heat, and stir the chicken and mushrooms into it.

7. Season the risotto with salt and pepper.

Now you have a meal fit for an ogre-tale.

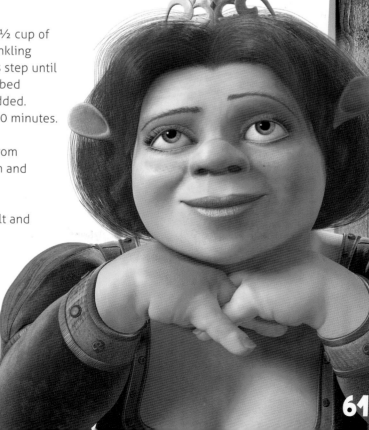

SHREK'S GREAT GOULASH

Once upon a time, Shrek cooked some weedrat, rotisserie style, for Fiona and she loved it. After the weedrat success Shrek was filled with cooking confidence and wanted to explore new dishes. The eager ogre looked through his recipes and in between swamp toad soup and fish-eye tartar he found a gourmet goulash dish that Fiona and the little ogres gobbled right up!

INGREDIENTS

2 tablespoons olive oil

½ cup diced yellow onion

1 cup white mushrooms, sliced

1 pound ground beef

3–4 medium bell peppers, seeded and diced

4 garlic cloves, chopped

Salt and ground black pepper to taste

¾ cup tomato paste

1½–2 cups water

1½ cups elbow macaroni

Fresh basil leaves, chopped

½–¾ cups grated mozzarella cheese (optional)

Serves 4
Prep time
20 min.
Cooking time
60 min.

INSTRUCTIONS

1. Heat the oil in a large pan over medium heat.

2. Add the onion and mushrooms, and cook them for 3–4 minutes, stirring gently.

3. Add the ground beef, bell peppers, and garlic to the pan. Season the meat and vegetables with salt and ground black pepper. Cook the mixture for 4-5 minutes, using a wooden spoon to crumble the beef as it cooks.

4. Drain any excess fat from the pan. Add the tomato paste and water to the beef, and stir until all the ingredients are evenly mixed. Simmer the sauce for 1–2 hours over low heat.

5. Cook the macaroni according to the package instructions then drain it well. Add the macaroni and basil to the sauce.

6. Gently stir the goulash until all the ingredients are well mixed. Then simmer it for 15 minutes over low heat.

7. Top the goulash with mozzarella cheese, if desired. Serve with bread and butter.

Shrek really knows how to beef up a goulash. The proof? It tastes even better on day two!

ALEX'S NEW YORK STRIP STEAK

The one meal Alex cannot forget—New York Strip Steak. The strip steak is a particularly tender cut of beef that has been associated with the city of New York since 1827. When Alex is far away from home on Madagascar, he can only dream of his favorite food!

INGREDIENTS

Herb Butter
¾ cup butter, slightly softened
½ cup dry parsley
2 tablespoons finely chopped chives
1 tablespoon dry thyme
¼ teaspoon ground black pepper
Salt to taste

Strip Steaks
1 tablespoon cooking oil
4 (9-ounce) beef strip steaks
Salt and ground black pepper to taste
Pat of butter

Serves 4
Prep time
30 min.
Cooking time
15-20 min.

INSTRUCTIONS

1. Prepare the herb butter by combining the butter, parsley, chives, thyme, pepper, and salt in a bowl. Stir the herbs and seasonings into the butter until evenly blended.

2. Spoon the herb butter onto a piece of plastic wrap. Loosely wrap the butter with the plastic and then roll it into a log. Chill the wrapped log in the freezer until firm, about 10 minutes.

3. To cook the steaks, heat the cooking oil in a heavy frying pan or cast iron skillet until smoking hot. Fry the steaks in the pan for 3–4 minutes on each side to brown them.

4. Reduce the heat to medium-low, and add the pat of butter to the pan. As the butter melts, carefully spoon it over the steaks while they continue to cook for 2 minutes.

5. Transfer the cooked steaks to a serving platter, and season them with salt and pepper.

6. Serve the steaks with pats of the herb butter, baked potatoes, and a small salad or your favorite vegetable.

Marty believes this dish—and being in the wild—is what really gives Alex his roar.

PENGUINS' PENGUINI

Status report: Skipper and his troops are stationed in Italy for reasons beyond Top Secret clearance. To keep their covert mission under wraps, Skipper declares 'Operation Penguin Blend-in.' This means doing what the locals do, like sharing gondola rides and shopping for spiffy leather bomber jackets. It also means eating what the locals eat, like the dish that's so good Skipper, Kowalski, Rico and Private risked everything to liberate the secret recipe once their mission was over...Prepare yourselves, boys, for Penguini.

INGREDIENTS

1½ cups chicken broth
17 sun-dried tomato halves
1 pound linguini
2 tablespoons olive oil
4 garlic cloves, minced
8 ounces white mushrooms, sliced
1 medium zucchini, chopped
13 small broccoli florets
¾ cup chopped fresh basil
1 cup grated Parmesan cheese

Serves 4
Prep time 10 min.
Cooking time 30 min.

INSTRUCTIONS

1. Bring the chicken broth to a boil in a small saucepan, then remove the pan from the heat.

2. Add the sun-dried tomatoes to the broth and let them stand until softened, about 20 minutes.

3. Use a slotted spoon to remove the tomatoes from the pan, and set the broth aside for now.

4. Thinly slice the tomatoes.

5. Cook the linguine in a large pot of boiling salted water, stirring occasionally, until the pasta is done but still firm to the bite. Drain the linguine and then return it to the pot.

6. Meanwhile, heat the oil in a large heavy pan over high heat. Fry the garlic in the oil for about 1 minute.

7. Carefully pour the reserved broth into the pan with the garlic. Then add the sun-dried tomatoes, mushrooms, zucchini, broccoli florets, and basil. Cook the mixture at a simmer for 3 minutes.

8. Add the vegetables to the pot of linguine, and gently toss them with the pasta.

9. Season the primavera with salt and pepper, and sprinkle Parmesan cheese on top.

Holy Butterballs! Could this be better than Cheezy Dibbles?

DRAGONFIRE PORK CHOPS

When the Vikings of Berk became friends with the dragons they quickly discovered how much help their winged comrades could be when it came to cooking. No more burning precious wood. Just throw meat on the fire pit and holler out to the nearest dragon. Next thing you know, you've got Dragonfire Pork Chops.

INGREDIENTS

1 cup canola oil
½ cup soy sauce
2 tablespoons Worcestershire sauce
2 garlic cloves, minced
1 tablespoon lemon juice
1 tablespoon yellow mustard
2 teaspoons dried parsley flakes
1 teaspoon ground black pepper
8 (4½-ounce) boneless center-cut pork chops
4 ears of corn, husked with the silk removed
4 pats of butter

Serves 4
Prep time 2 hrs.
Cooking time 30 min.

INSTRUCTIONS

1. Whisk together the canola oil, soy sauce, Worchestershire sauce, garlic, lemon juice, mustard, parsley, and pepper in a small mixing bowl. Pour the mixture into a sealable plastic bag.

2. Add the pork chops to the bag of marinade, tightly seal the bag, and place it in bowl (just in case it leaks). Chill the chops in the marinade for 1 hour or overnight.

3. When you're ready to cook the chops, drain and discard the marinade.

4. Cook the pork chops in a covered heavy frying pan over medium heat, flipping them midway through the cooking time, until they are thoroughly cooked, about 4–5 minutes per side. To test for doneness, stick the prongs of a fork into the center of the meat; the juice should be clear, not pink.

5. Transfer the cooked pork chops to a serving platter, and let them stand for 5 minutes before serving.

6. Meanwhile, bring a cup of lightly salted water to a boil in a clean frying pan. Reduce the heat, and use metal tongs to add the corn to the pan. Simmer the ears for 1½–2 minutes per side.

7. When the corn is ready, spread a pat of butter on each ear, and serve them with the pork chops.

Straight from the Viking cookeries of Berk, this sizzling supper is proof of just how helpful a well-trained dragon can be.

TILAPIA A LA HICCUP

What's worse than a ferocious dragon? A bored dragon. So one day when Toothless was too weary to wing, Hiccup added some spark to his routine. He challenged his Night Fury to a Flying Fish Fetch. Soon the fired-up dragon was nose-diving into icy waters for whatever fish he could fetch. How many fish? Too many. Now Hiccup had a huge challenge of his own: what to do with all that fish. Lucky for the Vikings that Hiccup is as inventive with dragon training as he is with supper.

INGREDIENTS

1 (46-ounce) can unsweetened
pineapple juice
¼ cup soy sauce
6 tablespoons olive oil
1 tablespoon grated fresh ginger
1 teaspoon hot sauce
1 teaspoon salt
Ground black pepper to taste
6 ounces tilapia fillets

Beet salad
14 ounces red or golden beets, peeled
¼ cup grated fresh horseradish
2 tablespoons lime juice
6 ounces plain yogurt
Salt and ground black pepper to taste

**Serves 4
Prep time
30 min.
Cooking time
50 min.**

INSTRUCTIONS

1. Bring the pineapple juice to a boil in a medium-size pot.

2. Add the soy sauce, reduce the heat, and simmer the juice for 20 minutes.

3. Remove the pan from the heat and let the liquid cool completely. Then add the oil, ginger, hot sauce, salt, and pepper.

4. Place the tilapia in a bowl, and pour the juice mixture over it. Cover the bowl and let the fish marinate in the refrigerator for 30–60 minutes.

5. Meanwhile, boil the beets in salted water for 30 minutes. Rinse the cooked beets and cut them into 1-inch cubes.

6. Mix together the beet cubes, horseradish, lime juice, and yogurt in a bowl. Season the salad with salt and pepper.

7. Preheat the oven to 350° F. Coat a baking dish with cooking spray.

8. Remove the tilapia from the marinade and place it in the baking dish. Discard the marinade. Bake the fish until it easily flakes apart with a fork, about 15–20 minutes.

9. Serve the tilapia with the beet salad on the side.

This fetching fish is sweet and tangy. The perfect dish to share with your friends and family, and even your dragon.

GUY'S FAMILY FEAST

Guy always has an answer because his head is full of ideas. His latest is spaghetti and meatballs for a crowd of Croods. But wait...what are spaghetti and meatballs? Eep thinks spaghetti makes cool ponytail holders. Sandy loves rolling meatballs underneath Gran's legs. For Grug, spaghetti sauce rocks a cave wall. Leave it to Guy to set the Croods straight: spaghetti and meatballs is a fun and tasty dinner. Dun, dun, duuuuuun!

INGREDIENTS

Meatballs
3 slices white bread with crusts
Milk – enough to cover the bread
1 pound ground beef
2 tablespoons Parmesan cheese, grated
2 large eggs, beaten
1 tablespoon dry parsley
1½ teaspoons dry oregano
1½ teaspoons dry thyme
1 large garlic clove, minced
1 teaspoon salt
½ teaspoon ground black pepper
2 tablespoons olive oil

Sauce and Spaghetti
2 teaspoons olive oil
½ cup yellow onion, chopped
2 green onions, chopped
2 teaspoons crushed garlic
1 (28-ounce) can peeled and diced tomatoes
4 teaspoons dry basil
4 teaspoons oregano
1 teaspoon white sugar
1 pound spaghetti
Grated Parmesan cheese

**Serves 4
Prep time 15 min.
Cooking time 35 min.**

5. Heat the oil in a large frying pan over medium heat. Fry the meatballs in the oil, turning them occasionally, until brown and cooked through, about 15 minutes. Set the meatballs and cooking juices aside.

6. To make the sauce, heat the oil in a large heavy saucepan over medium heat, and sauté the onion, green onion, and garlic in it.

7. When onions are glossy, stir in the tomatoes, basil, oregano, and sugar. Bring the mixture to a boil then reduce the heat to low and simmer the sauce for 20 minutes.

8. Add the meatballs and cooking juices to the saucepan, and continue to simmer the sauce for an additional 10 minutes.

9. Cook the spaghetti according to the package directions and then drain it. Toss the spaghetti with 1½ cups of the sauce in a large bowl.

10. Serve the spaghetti topped with meatballs, more sauce, and a sprinkling of Parmesan cheese.

Who knew cave cuisine could be so scrumptious!

INSTRUCTIONS

1. To make the meatballs, place the bread in a bowl and pour in enough milk to cover it. Let the bread stand for 10 minutes.

2. In a large bowl, combine the beef, Parmesan cheese, egg, parsley, oregano, thyme, garlic, salt, and pepper.

3. Squeeze the milk from the bread and then add the bread to the meat mixture. Blend well.

4. Use a tablespoon to shape the meat mixture into 24 meatballs.

73

SMEK'S HUMANSTOWN PIZZA

Smek is the wise leader of the Boov and he was very pleased with himself for finally finding their new home, Earth. It was the best planet yet! Among other things, Smek could not believe the vast variety of different food on this planet. He wanted to try everything, especially PIZZA! "Bring me a pizzathing!" he ordered.

INGREDIENTS

For this recipe it is perfectly fine to use ready-made pizza crust and pizza sauce.

Pizza sauce
1 can crushed tomatoes
2 tablespoons tomato paste
1 teaspoon oregano
1 teaspoon dried basil
½ teaspoon chili powder
2 teaspoons garlic powder
3 teaspoons onion powder
Salt and ground black pepper to taste

Pizza dough (for 3 small pizzas)
3¼–3½ cups all-purpose flour
1 package instant dry yeast
3 teaspoons course salt
1 cup lukewarm water
2 tablespoons vegetable oil

Toppings
1–2 cups grated mozzarella cheese
For pizza one: sliced pepperoni, olives, and mushrooms
For pizza two: diced ham and pineapple
For pizza three: thin tomato slices, extra-thick mozzarella slices, and whole basil leaves

**Serves 3-4
Prep time
80 min.
Cooking time
15-20 min.**

INSTRUCTIONS

1. Combine all of the sauce ingredients in the pitcher of a blender, and blend them until smooth. Set the sauce aside for now.

2. To make the pizza dough, gently stir together the flour, yeast, and salt in a large bowl.

3. Carefully stir the water and the oil into the flour mixture.

4. Knead the dough in the bowl until it pulls away from the sides. If the dough is too sticky, just mix in a little more flour.

5. Cover the bowl with plastic wrap, and set the dough in a warm place to rise for 1 hour.

6. When the dough is ready, preheat the oven to 450° F.

7. Divide the dough into three equal-size portions. Working with one portion at a time, shape the dough into a ball and then roll it out to the thickness you like. Be sure to sprinkle some flour on your working surface and the rolling pin first to keep the dough from sticking.

8. Transfer the rolled dough to a thin baking sheet or round pizza pan. (Tip: Sprinkling a little cornmeal on the sheet before adding the dough will help keep the crust from sticking when it bakes.)

9. Spread a thin layer of sauce on the pizza dough and then top it with a third of the mozzarella cheese.

10. Add your toppings of your choice. Remember, you don't need to pile them on. With pizza, a little goes a long way.

11. Bake each pizza until the cheese and crust has turned golden brown, at least 15 minutes or more. Slice the pizza into wedges to serve.

One, two, three incredible pizzas. What more do you need for a Boov-tastic dinner party?

DESSERTS

The Croods may not have a state-of-the-art kitchen—or even a modern home in which to put it. But it's pretty safe to say that they still enjoy preparing a hearty meal together, especially when it's topped off with something sweet.

CRANE'S FORTUNE COOKIES

Crane is a master of mindful existence. When it comes to making a dessert he is always thoughtful of the process it involves and the nature of the delicacy itself. The art of making a fortune cookie requires patience and a keen eye for detail. But once it is ready to eat, it is delicious. Just remember; stay focused and have fun.

INGREDIENTS

2 large egg whites
⅓ cup sugar
4 tablespoons butter, melted and cooled
½ cup flour
¼ teaspoon salt
½ teaspoon almond extract
½ teaspoon lemon extract
¼ cup ice-cold water

**Serves 4
Prep time
8 min.
Cooking time
5 min.**

INSTRUCTIONS

1. Preheat the oven to 350° F.

2. Write down all the fortunes you wish to insert in the cookies on a piece of clean paper. Cut out the fortunes and fold them so they are small enough to fits in a cookie.

3. Grease a cookie sheet thoroughly with cooking spray.

4. Whisk the egg whites in a large mixing bowl until light and foamy.

5. Blend in the sugar, melted butter, flour, salt, almond extract, and lemon extract. Mix the batter until well combined.

6. Mix in the ice water.

7. Drop 3 separate tablespoons of the batter onto the prepared cookie sheet, spacing them well apart. Use the back of the spoon to evenly spread each mound into a very thin 3-inch circle.

8. Bake the three cookies for 5–8 minutes or until the edges are a light golden color.

9. Working quickly and carefully, use a spatula to transfer one hot cookie at a time to a flat work surface, place a fortune atop the lower half, and fold the top over to form a semi-circle. Now, bend the folded cookie over the rim of a mug to turn it into a crescent shape. Immediately place the cookie in one of the cups of a mini muffin tin to hold its shape until it cools and crisps.

10. Repeat steps 7–9 until you've used all of the remaining batter and fortunes.

Remember, just as Po's dream of being a kung fu warrior came true, so can your own wishes for good fortune.

FIONA'S SWAMPY MUD PIE

It was Shrek and Fiona's first wedding anniversary. They were far away from home at the time and Fiona could see that Shrek was feeling a bit homesick. He was missing his swamp. Fiona wanted to do something special for her ogre hubby. Clever Fiona created this hearty homemade pie to remind Shrek of his swampy lair. Just like the swamp it's gooey and sticky. Unlike the swamp, it's delicious!

INGREDIENTS

Pie Shell
2 cups chocolate graham crackers
½ cup pecan halves
4 tablespoons butter

Pie Filling
⅔ cup granulated sugar
⅓ cup cocoa powder
⅓ cup cornstarch
¼ teaspoon salt
2½ cups milk
4 large egg yolks
1 teaspoon vanilla extract

Pie Topping
½ cup heavy cream
1 teaspoon granulated sugar
½ teaspoon vanilla extract

**Serves 8
Prep time
15 min.
Cooking time
120 min.**

INSTRUCTIONS

1. Preheat oven to 375° F.

2. To make the pie shell, finely crush or grind the graham crackers and pecans. Tip: An easy way to do this is to combine them in a sealed plastic bag and then roll over the bag with a rolling pin.

3. Melt the butter in a small saucepan over medium heat. Remove the pot from the heat, and carefully stir the crushed crackers and pecans into the melted butter until well blended.

4. Transfer the buttery crumbs into a 9-inch pie pan, and press them evenly against the bottom and up the sides.

5. Bake the pie shell for 8–10 minutes then let it cool completely.

6. When you're ready to make the filling, set a large sieve over the mouth of a medium bowl, and set the bowl aside for now.

7. Whisk together the sugar, cocoa powder, cornstarch, and salt in a medium-size heavy pot.

8. Whisk the milk into the cocoa mixture, a little at a time, being sure to incorporate the cornstarch. Now, whisk in the egg yolks.

9. Set the pot of cocoa mixture over medium heat, and whisk the contents constantly, watching carefully for the first bubbles to rise as the mixture comes to a boil. Lower the heat, and continue whisking while cooking the cocoa mixture at a gentle simmer for 1 minute.

10. Remove the pot from the heat, and immediately pour the chocolate filling through the sieve into the bowl.

11. Stir the vanilla extract and butter into the chocolate until well blended. Then pour the filling into the pie shell.

12. Cover the pie with plastic wrap, and chill it for at least 2 hours or, ideally, overnight.

13. Shortly before serving, make the whipped topping. In a chilled bowl, whisk together the cream, sugar, and vanilla extract until soft peaks form.

14. Spread the whipped cream over the pie.

This is the part where you eat the pie!

MARTY'S BIRTHDAY CAKE

Marty loves it when it's his birthday! Especially when he has such good friends like Alex, Gloria and Melman to help him celebrate. They never forget his birthday and always throw him a surprise party, with a cake and thoughtful gifts. This special cake is inspired by Marty's tenth birthday cake from the movie *Madagascar*. And it is crack-a-lackin'!

INGREDIENTS

1 cup almond flour
⅓ teaspoon salt
¾ cup granulated sugar
8 ounces dark baking chocolate
½ cup butter
6 large eggs
½ teaspoon vanilla extract
1 cup heavy cream
Strawberries or other fruit

**Serves 8
Prep time
30 min.
Cooking time
30-35 min.**

INSTRUCTIONS

1. Preheat the oven to 350° F.

2. Line the bottom of a 9-inch springform pan with parchment paper, and coat the bottom with vegetable cooking spray.

3. Whisk together the almond flour, salt, and 3 tablespoons of the sugar in a small bowl.

4. Carefully melt the chocolate and butter in a small heavy-bottomed pot over low heat, stirring frequently until they become a smooth sauce. Remove the pot from the heat to let the sauce cool slightly.

5. Whisk together the egg yolks and remaining sugar in a large bowl until the mixture is thick and pale yellow. Whisk in the vanilla extract.

6. Gently stir the chocolate into the egg mixture until well combined. Then stir the almond flour mixture into the batter.

7. In a separate large bowl, beat the egg whites until thick and creamy. Carefully fold the egg whites into the chocolate mixture until no white streaks remain.

8. Spread the batter evenly in the prepared pan, and bake it until the cake is set, about 30 to 35 minutes. Leave the cake in the pan to cool completely.

9. Transfer the cooled cake to a serving plate. Whisk the cream until stiff peaks form. Spoon the whipped cream onto the cake and top it with the fruit.

Fresh-a-licious!

83

THE MELMLOVA

Melman is a mild-mannered giraffe who sometimes stirs things up—in the kitchen. He simply stirs together some eggs and sugar, throws it in the oven, tosses a few succulent fruits on top, adds a dollop of whipped cream and—zoo-yah! A magnificent Melmlova is ready for his friends to devour.

INGREDIENTS

4 large egg whites

1 cup plus 2 tablespoons granulated sugar

3 cups heavy cream, whipped

Mixed fruit

Serves 8
Prep time
45 min.
Cooking time
2-3 hrs.

INSTRUCTIONS

1. Preheat the oven to 250° F.

2. Using a stand mixer on medium speed, whisk the egg whites until light and foamy.

3. Add the sugar little by little to blend it into the egg whites. Continue whipping the mixture until stiff peaks form. This is called meringue.

4. Line a baking sheet with parchment paper. Pour the meringue onto the paper, starting in the middle of the sheet, and letting it level itself.

5. Bake the meringue in the oven until it is cooked through and dry, but still white, about 2–3 hours.

6. Let the meringue cool completely. Then top it with the whipped cream and fruit.

For Melman, baking isn't just fun, it's what the doctor ordered.

ASTRID'S APPLE CAKE

Life can be pretty sweet for Hiccup and the Dragon Riders of Berk. So after a busy day of dragon training, high-flying adventures and exploring new worlds, a sweet snack is what they crave. Enter Astrid with her home-baked, mouth-watering apple cake. Turns out Astrid is as cunning in the kitchen as she is battling bad guys.

INGREDIENTS

1¾ cups all-purpose flour
1 teaspoon baking powder
¼ teaspoon salt
¾ cup butter, softened
1 cup granulated sugar
3 large eggs
½ cup heavy cream
2 teaspoons vanilla extract
2 Granny Smith apples, peeled, cored, and sliced
2–3 tablespoons cinnamon sugar

**Serves 8
Prep time
45 min.
Cooking time
45 min.**

INSTRUCTIONS

1. Preheat the oven to 350° F. Coat the inner bottom and sides of a 9-inch springform pan with cooking spray.

2. Whisk together the flour, baking powder, and salt in a small bowl.

3. Combine the butter and sugar in a larger mixing bowl, and use an electric mixer to beat them together until light. Beat in the eggs one at a time.

4. Gradually beat the flour mixture into the butter mixture.

5. Now mix in the cream and vanilla extract just until blended. It's important not to over-whip the batter once the cream is added.

6. Pour the batter into the prepared pan.

7. Scatter the apple slices atop the batter and then sprinkle on the cinnamon sugar.

8. Bake the cake for 45 minutes. Then let it cool in the pan before unmolding it.

Be warned—this irresistible dessert won't last long in a village of dragon trainers.

RUFF 'N' TUFF CHOCOLATE CHIP COOKIES

Ruffnut and Tuffnut are one pair of whacky twins. Although stubborn, tough and mischievous trouble makers, they can be surprisingly clever. And like most twins they share everything, from their Hideous Zippleback dragon to their favorite treat—cookies. With two cups bursting with chocolate, Ruff 'n' Tuff's cookies are double the fun and the yum.

INGREDIENTS

2¼ cups all-purpose flour
1 teaspoon baking soda
1 teaspoon salt
1 cup butter, softened
¾ cup granulated sugar
¾ cup brown sugar
1 teaspoon vanilla extract
2 large eggs
2 cups chopped semisweet dark chocolate or packaged morsels

**Serves 8
Prep time
30 min.
Cooking time
12-16 min.**

INSTRUCTIONS

1. Preheat the oven to 375° F.

2. Combine the flour, baking soda, and salt in a small bowl.

3. In a separate mixing bowl, combine the butter, granulated sugar, brown sugar, and vanilla extract. Use an electric mixer to beat the mixture until well combined and creamy. Mix in the eggs one at a time.

4. Blend the flour mixture into the butter mixture. Then stir the chopped dark chocolate into the dough.

5. Drop tablespoonfuls of the dough onto ungreased baking sheets, spacing them evenly apart.

6. Bake the cookies until they turn golden brown, about 9–11 minutes.

7. Transfer the baked cookies to wire racks to cool.

Ruffnut and Tuffnut may bicker about everything else, but when it comes to their favorite treat, they're in total accord. A batch of their namesake cookies is always first choice!

PUNCH MONKEY BANANA BREAD

You'd have to be living in a cave not to know Punch Monkey's love bananas. They love them high in trees. They love them upside down. They even love them flung in the air and gulped down whole. But will the monkeys love them baked inside a sweet, warm banana bread? You betcha. Because this dish totally packs a punch...of flavor.

INGREDIENTS

1½ cups all-purpose flour
1 teaspoon baking soda
¼ teaspoon salt
¼ cup whole milk
3½ tablespoons butter
2 large eggs
1 cup sugar
2 ripe bananas
1 teaspoon vanilla extract

**Serves 8
Prep time
45 min.
Cooking time
60-85 min.**

INSTRUCTIONS

1. Preheat the oven to 350° F. Spray the inside of a loaf pan with cooking spray.

2. Sift together the flour, baking soda, and salt in a small bowl. Set the mixture aside.

3. Heat the milk in a small saucepan over low heat. Turn off the heat, and add the butter, letting it melt in the milk.

4. Using an electric mixer, whisk together the eggs and sugar in a mixing bowl until light and fluffy.

5. Mash the bananas in a separate bowl. Mix the mashed banana and vanilla extract into the egg mixture.

6. Stir the flour mixture into the egg-and-banana mixture.

7. Fill the prepared loaf pan with the batter.

8. Bake the banana bread until a toothpick inserted in the center comes out clean, about 60–85 minutes.

Eat up! You never know when Punch Monkey may snatch the last piece of banana bread from your plate.

MYMOM'S MILKSHAKE

When Tip wanted to give Oh a taste of life on planet Earth she knew where to start: with a tall glass of the creamy milkshake her mom likes to make. At first Oh was reluctant. How did a milkshake taste? Like those gas station blue mints? Or that lemonade in that weird-looking bowl? No way! One sip of this sweet milkshake was enough to make Oh jump and shake his Boov-thing.
No wonder they call it a milkshake!

INGREDIENTS

Serves 3
Prep time 10 min.

4½ cups vanilla ice cream

1¼ cups milk

¾ cup pineapple juice

Colored sprinkles

INSTRUCTIONS

1. Pour the milk and pineapple juice into the pitcher of a blender. Add the ice cream.

2. Blend the mixture thoroughly.

3. Pour the milkshake into a large glass, and decorate the top with colored sprinkles.

Tip's mom's milkshake recipe can only be described as Oh, so delicious!

INDEX

INDEX

INDEX